100% Alkaline Vegan Smoothies

Delicious, Alkaline Cleanse-Friendly Superfood Smoothies for Healing and Natural Weight Loss

Copyright ©Karen Greenvang 2019

All rights reserved. No part of this publication may be reproduced, stored in a retrieval system, or transmitted, in any form or by any means, electronic, mechanical, photocopying, recording or otherwise, without the prior written permission of the author and the publishers.

The scanning, uploading, and distribution of this book via the Internet, or via any other means, without the permission of the author is illegal and punishable by law. Please purchase only authorized electronic editions, and do not participate in or encourage electronic piracy of copyrighted materials.

All information in this book has been carefully researched and checked for factual accuracy. However, the author and publishers make no warranty, expressed or implied, that the information contained herein is appropriate for every individual, situation or purpose, and assume no responsibility for errors or omission. The reader assumes the risk and full responsibility for all actions, and the author will not be held liable for any loss or damage, whether consequential, incidental, and special or otherwise, that may result from the information presented in this publication.

All cooking is an experiment in a sense, and many people come to the same or similar recipe over time. All recipes in this book have been derived from author's personal experience. Should any bear a close resemblance to those used elsewhere, that is purely coincidental.

The book is not intended to provide medical advice or to take the place of medical advice and treatment from your personal physician. Readers are advised to consult their own doctors or other qualified health professionals regarding the treatment of medical conditions. The author shall not be held liable or responsible for any misunderstanding or misuse of the information contained in this book. The information is not intended to diagnose, treat or cure any disease.

It is important to remember that the author of this book is not a doctor/ medical professional. Only opinions based upon her own personal experiences or research are cited. THE AUTHOR DOES NOT OFFER MEDICAL ADVICE or prescribe any treatments. For any health or medical issues – you should be talking to your doctor first.

Contents

Ready to Transform Your Wellbeing?..............................10

Recipe #1 Creamy Alkaline Smoothie for Balance and Energy 40

Recipe #2 Alkaline Vegan Fill Me Up Smoothie 41

Recipe #3 Natural Beauty Alkaline Smoothie 42

Recipe #4 Repair Your Beautiful Cells Smoothie 43

Recipe#5 Create Massive Balance Alkaline Smoothie 45

Recipe#6 Clean Liver Happy Mind Alkaline Smoothie 47

Recipe#7 Detox Your Body, Mind, and Soul Alkaline Smoothie 48

Recipe#8 Alkaline Vegan Keto Health Freak Smoothie 49

Recipe #9 Sweet But Super Alkaline Smoothie 50

Recipe #10 Vitamin C Happy Mind Smoothie 51

Recipe #11 Alkaline Mediterranean Smoothie Meal . 52

Recipe #12 Sexy Chia Seed Smoothie 54

Recipe #13 Spicy Alkaline Smoothie Meal Replacement 55

Recipe #14 Quinoa Alkaline Protein Smoothie 57

Recipe #15 Spicy Green Aphrodisiac Smoothie 59

Recipe #16 When Life Throws Lemons Smoothie 60

Recipe #17 Irresistible Satisfaction Smoothie 61

Recipe #18 Sweet Sleep Princess Alkaline Smoothie .63

Recipe #19 Herbs Are Awesome Smoothie 64

Recipe #20 Creamy Glow Alkaline Smoothie 65

Recipe #21 Anti-Inflammatory Power Alkaline Smoothie..66

Recipe #22 Sweet Herbal Dream Alkaline Smoothie .68

Recipe #23 Rooibos Energy Smoothie 69

Recipe #24 Veggies Taste Awesome Smoothie 70

Recipe #25 Fill Me Up Easy Lunch Smoothie 71

Recipe #26 No-Guilt Healthy Alkaline Vegan Treat Smoothie..73

Recipe #27 Relax Your Body, Mind, and Soul Smoothie 74

Recipe #28 The New Spanish Alkaline Smoothie 75

Recipe #29 Super Effective Detox Smoothie 76

Recipe #30 Cinnamon Aphrodisiac Smoothie.............77

Recipe #31 Hydration Refreshment Alkaline Protein Smoothie..78

Recipe #32 Easy Sweet Green Smoothie 79

Special Offer from Karen- VIP Reader Newsletter 84

More Books by Karen Greenvang 86

Scientific Resources 98

Introduction

Introduction

Ready to Transform Your Wellbeing?

Thank you so much for taking an interest in this book.
My name is Karen, and I write easy-to-follow vegan-friendly recipe books to help people live a healthier and more conscious lifestyle.

This book is very special to me as it fuses the best of the vegan and alkaline diets to give you an easy to follow smoothie blueprint for fantastic energy and vibrant health.

Wait? Isn't vegan the same as alkaline?

This is the exact question I get asked so often. Before my vegan and health journey, I used to think that alkaline was the same as a vegan (or plant-based). And yes, these 2 concepts very often overlap.

But, the philosophy behind them is a bit different. Please read with an open mind, my purpose is NOT to judge your dietary or lifestyle choices. My only goal behind my books is to provide you with easy to follow information and practical tips and recipes so

Introduction

that you can try them for yourself to see what really works for you. Everyone is different.

With that being said, let's start with a vegan diet. The main goal behind it is to abstain from eating all kinds of animal products followed by an animal-product free lifestyle (no leather, no animal-tested beauty products, etc.). The motivation that all ethical vegans have in common is to end animal suffering.

A vegan diet can be super healthy and balanced, or processed and unbalanced. The mere fact that something is vegan-friendly, does not necessarily mean it's good for you (although it can be).

And yes, I am a vegan writing this! I need to confess to you- when I first got started on my vegan journey, I was an unhealthy, lazy, processed-food-addict vegan. Yes, I did feel good as far as my "no more animal products" mindset was concerned. And I was happy I was acting in alignment with my new choices.

Unfortunately, I did not follow a vegan diet properly. I did not eat enough, and the quality of my calories was very poor due to my relying mostly on

Introduction

processed, unhealthy vegan products, too much sugar, unhealthy oils, and all the vegan junk food.

That was a wakeup call for me, as I started to feel more and more tired. Many people (including my doctors) wanted me to go back to eating animal products; however, I decided to do my own research instead. I quickly realized that my vegan diet was not healthy and balanced, and if I wanted to stick to it and feel good at the same time, I had to learn a bit more about nutrition so that I could shift from processed vegan junk food to a super healthy vegan diet. And I need to be honest with you, my dear reader! It was (and still is) lots of work. But I do enjoy the journey!

My journey led me to discover a clean, wholefood, plant-based diet. I would track what I ate. It worked well. I also visited a plant-based nutritionist and a naturopathic doctor who said I could follow a vegan diet and be healthy. That was good news for me!

I got a couple of supplements and a ton of motivation to experiment with a healthy version of vegan-friendly dieting. That led me to a plant-based

Introduction

diet. A wholefood, super healthy, unprocessed plant-based diet.

As I was exploring a plant-based diet community, I noticed that unlike in the case of a vegan diet, most people's motivation was based around improving their own health. Some people in that plant-based community also happened to be vegan, as me.

But some were interested in a whole-food, plant-based lifestyle as a natural medicine to ease their pain or prevent some diseases.

It was an interesting observation for me at that time. Please note- I do not bash people for not being a vegan for "vegan purposes" (animals). Before becoming a vegan, I was a meat-eater for many years, so who am I to judge?

My audience that is people who read my books are not all 100% vegan-based. Some are, and some are mostly plant-based and are interested in learning simple, vegan-friendly plant-based recipes for different reasons. But those who are already on a vegan lifestyle, understand that to maintain it, they also need to take care of their health.

Introduction

So, there you have it. A plant-based whole food diet is like a super healthy and clean approach to a vegan diet that excludes all the nasty, processed stuff.

Pretty simple.

So, what the heck is an alkaline diet? Isn't it the same as a vegan or plant-based diet?

Well, some parts of it are. But, in its pure form, the alkaline diet is much more hardcore and a bit narrower than a plant-based diet (although many concepts overlap).

In other words, not all vegan or even wholefood plant-based foods are alkaline. However, all alkaline-friendly foods are vegan.

If you have ever researched the alkaline diet, you may have gotten a headache. All that pH stuff is so complicated. Not only that…Then, you search for food lists online, and it looks like different alkaline experts have different opinions. And so, it becomes even more confusing! Luckily, after studying a ton of alkaline books and courses, I was able to come up with a simple, comprehensive, super alkaline-rich

Introduction

food list that was a foundation for my strictly alkaline (and vegan) recipes I created to share with you in this book.

But...before we get into the food lists and recipes...what is an alkaline diet actually? Is it about changing your body's pH?

Can you make your body more alkaline?

Well, you actually can't.

<u>The alkaline diet is not about "making your body more alkaline.</u>" Statements like this one only get an alkaline diet, a terrible rep, especially in medical environments. Therefore, there are so many alkaline diet skeptics who call this diet *some pseudo-science*.

But, you will also find a ton of health success stories based on alkaline diets...However, real health success takes commitment, passion, and motivation. There are no magic cures. Creating vibrant health through balanced nutrition is a process. Alkaline foods are a great tool you can use on your health journey, but you need to promise yourself to be patient and

Introduction

courageous enough to stick with it (like anything else in life, good stuff takes some time).

As a health-conscious person, I would also encourage you to do regular checkups with your physician as well as regular blood work. You need to track your progress. <u>Most people skip it or overlook it.</u> But your health foundation is in the data. My most significant health shift happened when I began investing in naturopathic doctors and qualified nutritionists who could look at my data (such as blood work) and give me some personalized advice. Yea, it was a bit expensive. But anyone who has been through any serious health issues understands that vibrant health is the foundation of EVERYTHING we do. With more energy, health, and mental wellbeing, it's so much easier to find more work, improve your skills, or do anything you need to do to make more money. The hardest thing to make is health. Some say- health is wealth. I say- health is life, and lack of health means death. Anyways...

So how does it work? Can you make your body "more alkaline"?

Introduction

Yes, in an alkaline community, we very often say things like "Let's alkalize" and whatnot, but the meaning behind it is simply- let's eat more alkaline foods. The saying: "let's get alkaline or let's alkalize" should not be interpreted too directly.

Because the alkaline diet is not about making yourself more alkaline. Your body already does everything for you. Also, some parts of your body, like, for example, your stomach, is actually meant to be acidic.

Introduction

How the Alkaline Diet Actually Works (not what you think)

So, here is how it works (very, very simple). Also, at the end of this book, I have included some scientific proof, in case you are interested in diving deep and in all the "why."

This book focuses on the "How," but if you are like me, and you are a curious soul, I am sure you will appreciate my extra work and effort by adding some additional resources at the end of this booklet for your investigation. For the purpose of this little book, I make it super easy and straightforward to follow.

The pH of most of our crucial cellular and other body fluids, like blood, is designed to be at a pH of 7.365, which is slightly alkaline.

Your body has an intricate system in place to maintain that healthy, slightly alkaline pH level.

However, to make it work at the optimal level, you need to ensure you eat a healthy, balanced, unprocessed diet rich in alkaline-forming foods.

Introduction

If you focus on unhealthy choices, for example, the Standard Western Diet with its overload of sugars, processed carbohydrates, dairy, soda, too many animal products, and fast food we make it more and more difficult for our body to regulate our optimal pH and enjoy natural energy (and optimal health). A processed vegan diet (full of yeast, processed carbs, sugars, and other nasty chemicals) is also not the best way to go about your health.

The Dangers of a Crappy Vegan Diet (been guilty!)

"Yes, I no longer eat meat and animal products, Karen!" – cool, I am happy to hear that!

But what about what you do-do eat? What I am writing about here is very important as this approach very often gives a vegan diet/vegan community a bad rep. *"Oh, I went vegan, and I feel like crap"- well, it's probably because you did a processed vegan diet, not a healthy, balanced, whole food vegan diet rich in living, alkaline foods…*

Introduction

Once again (no more rants, I promise!)

The pH of most of our crucial cellular and other body fluids, like blood, is designed to be at a pH of 7.365, which is slightly alkaline.

Your body has an intricate system in place to maintain that healthy, slightly alkaline pH level.

The main focus of the alkaline diet is to give your body the nourishment and the healing tools that it needs to MAINTAIN that optimal pH almost effortlessly.

By eating an unhealthy, processed food diet, we make our body work "overtime." It will work harder and harder to keep balancing our pH at the risk of succumbing to disease. Oh, and by eating an "anti-alkaline" processed food diet, you will be experiencing very low energy levels as well as low focus and concentration.

I have been there myself, and I don't want to go back there again!

Introduction

So, back to comparing alkaline diet to a vegan diet or a whole food plant-based diet...if you are already eating a healthy, balanced unprocessed vegan or plant-based diet, chances are, you are already eating pretty alkaline (it will all make sense when we dive into the foods lists and the recipes).

As I was researching an alkaline diet, I also came across the term "alkalarian" used by many alkaline diet experts and followers.

I also noticed that some alkaline diet followers were vegan or "plant-based terians" and some were on what I would call an "almost plant-based" diet (adding in a bit of fish or eggs).

And so, not alkaline diet followers are automatically vegans. But many vegans can be automatically alkaline (unless they eat lots of processed vegan junk food as I used to).

The hardcore alkaline diet, is much more restrictive than a simple, balanced whole food plant-based diet, as it also excludes most fruits (basically all high sugar fruits), mushrooms, fermented foods, and some alkaline experts even exclude healthy algae.

Introduction

Coffee and tea are vegan and plant-based friendly and, if used in small amounts, in moderation, it's OK. But not on a strictly alkaline diet, where all the caffeine sources are off.

I know what you are thinking right now! "Karen, what are you getting me into?". I used to say the exact same thing.

And I asked myself…would it be possible for me to eat 100% alkaline all the time?

Well, even as a vegan and healthy, plant-based diet follower and someone who is already "seasoned" in this health and wellness world, I kept asking myself this question all the time, and eventually, I reached out to several alkaline diet experts, authors, bloggers, and nutritionists.

And I loved what I found. They all pointed out the so-called 80/20 rule. Some even said that 70/30 is okay if I am already living a healthy plant-based lifestyle and haven't had an animal product in a long time.

And so, I switched my diet to a more alkaline direction (roughly ¾ alkaline and the rest, still

Introduction

healthy and plant-based but not strictly alkaline), and it worked great. After a few weeks of following a vegan-plant-based-alkaline combo, I felt much more energized.

Everyone around me has been asking me what I have been doing. The first question was, "Wow Karen, this vegan thing must be working, I am gonna go vegan too".

Needless to say, I am always delighted to inspire people to go vegan, whatever their reasons may be. But I knew it was more than just a vegan diet , and I knew it was more than just a whole food plant-based diet.

It was the effect of alkaline foods...especially the right alkaline foods! So, my recipe was – healthy vegan alkaline mix!

For example, I used to drink a ton of banana smoothies, thinking that bananas were alkaline fruits. I found several online charts listing bananas as alkaline fruits.

Introduction

But, after diving deeper into alkaline fruits, I learned that only low-sugar fruits are strictly alkaline. Does it mean I fear bananas? Nope, I still eat them as a part of my non-alkaline diet. But now, I focus more on alkaline fruits and other alkaline-friendly foods.

Ready for the best part? It's very easy to tell what is alkaline or not.

For example, bananas are rich in alkaline minerals such as Magnesium or Potassium. But, they are also rich in sugar, and because of that, they are not alkaline-forming (because everything with sugar in it, even natural, has an acidic effect on your body once metabolized).

Now, I still do some banana smoothies, but I also add in some greens and alkaline fruits to create balance.

I want to make it as clear as possible- I don't fear fruit, and I don't eat 100% alkaline. I eat 100% vegan plant-based and 70%-80% alkaline. So please don't get too paranoid (balance is key). Also-. Different strokes for different folks. Your vegan-alkaline combo, or alkaline-something combo (if you are not vegan) may be different than mine.

Introduction

Many things will also depend on your athletic activity. A 100% alkaline diet is very low-carb in its design. Personally, I can't live on a low carb diet, it makes me very anxious.

At the same time, I can't live on a super high carb diet either (if it works for you- do it!). I focus on balance- something in between low and high carb is what works for me and my athletic activity (which is moderate but consistent, no I am not on my bike for 8 hours a day like most online vegans out there, but I do hit the gym 6 days a week for 1, max 2 hours, and the work I do is sedentary).

OK, so which fruits are strictly alkaline?
All low-sugar fruits, such as:
-limes
-lemons
-grapefruits
-avocados
-pomegranates
-tomatoes

These are all rich in alkaline minerals but low in sugar at the same time. Yes, limes and lemons are alkaline. And so are grapefruits.

Introduction

Oranges contain more sugar, which makes them less alkaline to the body.

So, what do all alkaline foods have in common?
-they are very low in sugar (such as alkaline fruits listed above)
-they are rich in vitamins and minerals
-they are plant-based and unprocessed
-they are not fermented
-most of them are rich in chlorophyll
-they do not contain caffeine

As I said, I eat a balanced plant-based diet where about 70% of my diet is alkaline foods.

However, once or twice a year, I like to do an alkaline cleanse, and I would love to inspire you to do it too.

An alkaline cleanse is when you go entirely- strictly alkaline for a week or two. Yes, hardcore alkaline. The main goal is to give your body a break and reset. While it would be tough to be 100% strictly alkaline for an extended period (although it makes sense in clinical settings under naturopathic doctor's supervision in some instances), it makes total sense if you intend to cleanse, nourish and reset your body.

Introduction

Then, I get back to my "normal" clean food plant-based diet (the 70/30, or 80/20 rule).

In my other book, *Alkaline Vegan Drinks*, most recipes take a balanced 80/20 or 70/30 approach. This book, however, focuses on 100% alkaline cleanse friendly recipes.

Whenever I go on an alkaline cleanse, I focus mostly on smoothies, with some juices and soups and salads in between.

The hardest thing for me is always- caffeine...but I still do my regular cleansing, and eventually, it helps me find more inner peace, discipline, and personal power. Yes, a little bit of tea or coffee is OK on a balanced plant-based diet...but not allowed on a strict alkaline diet (or alkaline cleanse).

If your goal is to do an alkaline-cleanse, make sure you eat enough calories (it's not a juice or water cleanse, you need to eat and drink right, nourishing "alkaline calories" to help your body get back into balance).

Introduction

You may also discuss such a cleanse with your physician or a naturopathic doctor, especially if you are on medication or under doctor's care (or recovering from any severe health issues).

The recipes from this book can be used for any alkaline-friendly cleanse or to supplement your healthy diet. Many of my friends (some vegan some not) tried my recipes to lose weight. They all had one of my strictly alkaline-vegan smoothies for breakfast (followed by a moderately alkaline but definitely clean food diet), and they all began losing weight naturally without stressing too much about it.

Most of them got so much energy that going to a gym or for a walk was no longer a problem. Heck, one of my friends, started waking up at 5 and writing novels, which always was a passion of his. All while working in a full-time job and playing with his kids in the evening (and working out at his lunch break).

How much would your life change if you could increase your energy levels? What about that old passion of yours you have always wanted to do?

Introduction

It feels so good to share this information, because I have seen many people transform, just by eating more alkaline (in this case- drinking more alkaline smoothies).

So, you can use this book, however you want! Either for a cleanse or to support and complement any healthy diet of your choice (just be sure to make around ¾ of your diet rich in alkaline foods for optimal benefits).

Introduction

Also, if you enjoyed this intro, be sure to join my free, safe, spam-free mailing lists for more vegan-plant-based-alkaline health tips and recipes:

https://www.yourwellnessbooks.com/karen

I send out valuable emails once (maximum twice) a week, and I honor your email-space. I do not send out any annoying mass marketing emails. Whenever I publish a new book, you will surely get it at a massive discount because I want to make sure you benefit from my information as much as possible.

And, if for some reason you don't like my emails, I make it easy to unsubscribe. I am not some big faceless corporation, but a normal human being, on the same journey as you are.

Any problems with your sign up, please email me at karen@yourwellnessbooks.com

Introduction

Now, let's have a look at the alkaline food lists for our smoothies, shall we?

(please note, at the end of this book, I included comprehensive alkaline-acid food charts for your journey, but since it's a smoothie book, we are focusing mostly on alkaline smoothie food lists)

Alkaline-Friendly Smoothie Ingredients

Alkaline Beverages and Liquids
-Filtered Alkaline Water
-Herbal, Caffeine-Free infusions
-Lemon juice (fresh)
-Grapefruit Juice (fresh)
-Pomegranate Juice
-Vegetable Juice (fresh)
-fresh coconut water (unsweetened, no preservatives)

Vegan Alkaline milk (make sure it's unsweetened and organic with no nasty stuff added)
-coconut milk
-cashew milk
-almonds milk
-quinoa milk
-chia seed milk

Nuts and seeds:
-almonds
-fennel seeds
-cashews
-cardamon seeds
-pine nuts
-macadamia nuts
-pumpkin seeds

Alkaline-Friendly Smoothie Ingredients

-chia seeds

+Healthy gluten-free grains such as **quinoa** can be added to smoothies to fill you up

Alkaline Fruit:
-avocado
-coconut
-grapefruit
-limes
-tomatoes
-pomegranates

All fresh veggies and greens you can possibly add to your smoothies:
-All leafy greens- spinach, kale, arugula…
-cucumber
-zucchini
-cauliflower
-broccoli
-red, green and yellow bell peppers
-carrots
-fresh cilantro leaves
-fresh parsley leaves

Alkaline-Friendly Smoothie Ingredients

All herbs and spices such as:
-curry (great for spicy veggie smoothies)
-cinnamon (great for naturally sweet smoothies)
-nutmeg
-vanilla

Other:
-nori seaweed
-Himalayan salt
-stevia (use very sparingly though)
-organic spirulina powder
-organic chlorella powder

Healthy oils such as:
-avocado oil
-Olive oil
-Coconut oil
-Flaxseed oil

Alkaline-Friendly Smoothie Ingredients

The alkaline smoothie list seems pretty short and straightforward, because we are focusing only super alkaline ingredients. However, the possibilities are endless.

You can make delicious, creamy, naturally sweet smoothies…

Or, green, vegetable spicy smoothies, you can serve as a quick detox soup.

This guide will show you how to use spices in your smoothies to make them taste amazing!

Now, let's get down to blending…

Measurements Used in the Recipes

The cup measurement I use is the American Cup measurement.

I also use it for dry ingredients. If you are new to it, let me help you:

If you don't have American Cup measures, just use a metric or imperial liquid measuring jug and fill your jug with your ingredient to the corresponding level. Here's how to go about it:

1 American Cup= 250ml= 8 fl.oz.
For example:
If a recipe calls for 1 cup of almonds, simply place your almonds into your measuring jug until it reaches the 250 ml/8oz marks.

Quite easy, right?

I know that different countries use different measurements, and I wanted to make things simple for you. I have also noticed that very often, those who are used to American Cup measurements complain about metric measurements and vice versa. However, if you apply what I have just explained, you will find it easy to use both.

100% Alkaline Smoothie Recipes

Recipe #1 Creamy Alkaline Smoothie for Balance and Energy

The smoothie is naturally creamy and very tasty. The cinnamon powder makes this smoothie nice and sweet. Coconut oil will help you reduce sugar cravings.

Serves: 1-2
Ingredients
Liquid:
- 2 cups cold coconut milk, unsweetened
- 1 tablespoon coconut oil
- 2 tablespoons fresh lime juice

Dry:
- 1 small avocado, peeled and pitted
- A handful of cashews, raw, soaked in filtered water for at least a few hours
- 1 tablespoon chia seeds

Other:
- 1 teaspoon cinnamon powder
- Half teaspoon ginger powder
- Optional- stevia to sweeten

Instructions
1. Blend all the ingredients using a blender.
2. Process until smooth.
3. Serve and enjoy! This nutritious smoothie makes a great breakfast.

Recipe #2 Alkaline Vegan Fill Me Up Smoothie

This alkaline-vegan smoothie tastes a bit like Greek yogurt but is entirely plant-based and dairy-free.

Serves: 1-2
Ingredients
Liquid:
- 2 cups cold unsweetened almond milk
- 1 tablespoon avocado oil

Dry:
- 2 tablespoons chia seeds (or chia seed powder)
- 1 small lemon, peeled and sliced
- 1 small avocado, peeled and pitted

Other:
- a few lime slices to garnish
- a pinch of Himalayan salt
- a pinch of black pepper to taste

Instructions
1. Place all the ingredients in a blender.
2. Blend until smooth. Serve and enjoy!

Recipe #3 Natural Beauty Alkaline Smoothie

This alkaline vegan smoothie is designed to help you have a super healthy-looking, glowing skin while increasing your energy levels at the same time!

Serves: 1-2
Ingredients
Liquid:
- 1 cup cashew milk
- Half cup of coconut water

Dry:
- 2 small carrots, peeled
- 1 big red bell pepper, cut into smaller pieces
- 2 tablespoons chia seeds

Other:
- 1 teaspoon cinnamon powder
- stevia to sweeten if needed
- fresh mint leaves and lime slices to serve

Instructions
1. Place all the ingredients in a blender.
2. Blend until smooth.
3. Pour into a glass and enjoy!

Recipe #4 Repair Your Beautiful Cells Smoothie

If you want to transition to making super healthy alkaline vegan smoothies, you gotta explore moringa, mint, and cilantro! Moringa is a natural protein alkaline superfood. It contains all the essential amino acids – the building blocks of protein- that are needed to grow, repair, and maintain cells. At the same time, it's rich in alkaline-forming minerals such as magnesium, iron, and potassium.

Serves: 1-2
Ingredients
Liquid:
- 1 cup of coconut milk
- Half cup fresh grapefruit juice

Dry:
- Handful almonds, soaked in filtered water for at least a few hours
- 1-inch fresh ginger, peeled
- A few avocado slices

Other:
- 1 teaspoon moringa powder
- A handful of fresh mint washed
- A handful of fresh cilantro leaves washed

Instructions
1. Place all the ingredients into a blender
2. Process well until smooth. Enjoy!

Recipe#5 Create Massive Balance Alkaline Smoothie

This smoothie is perfect as a quick detox smoothie to help you enjoy more energy!

Servings: 2-3
Ingredients
Liquid:
- 1 cup almond milk
- Half cup water, filtered, preferably alkaline
- 1 tablespoon coconut oil

Dry:
- 2 big cucumbers, peeled and roughly sliced
- 1 big avocado
- Half lemon, peeled and sliced
- 4 tablespoons almonds, chopped or powdered
- A handful of cilantro
- 1 tablespoon almond or hemp seed protein powder

Other:
- Pinch of Himalaya salt to taste
- Pinch of black pepper to taste
- 2 tablespoons chive, chopped
- 1 teaspoon spirulina powder

Instructions:
1. Place all the ingredients in a blender.
2. Blend well and pour into a smoothie glass or a small soup bowl.
3. Serve and enjoy!

Recipe#6 Clean Liver Happy Mind Alkaline Smoothie

If you want to improve your energy levels, consider doing a mini liver cleanse. This recipe is just perfect as a quick breakfast smoothie to help you take care of your liver first thing in the morning.

Servings: 1-2
Ingredients
Liquid:
- 1 cup full-fat coconut milk (no added sugar)
- Half cup of water, filtered, preferably alkaline

Dry:
- Half cup radish washed
- 1 small avocado, peeled and pitted
- A handful of fresh arugula leaves

Other:
- Pinch of Himalaya salt to taste
- 1 teaspoon spirulina

Instructions:
1. Blend all the ingredients.
2. Serve and enjoy!

Recipe#7 Detox Your Body, Mind, and Soul Alkaline Smoothie

Cilantro is a miraculous alkaline herb with potent antioxidant properties. It tastes great in smoothies!

Servings: 2-3
Ingredients
Liquid:
- 2 cups coconut milk
- 1 tablespoon coconut oil

Dry:
- A handful of fresh cilantro leaves
- 2 small carrots, peeled

Other:
- half teaspoon ginger
- 1 teaspoon moringa
- Half teaspoon cinnamon powder
- Pinch of Himalaya salt to taste

Instructions:
1. Combine all the ingredients in a blender.
2. Process until smooth.
3. Pour into a smoothie glass or a small soup bowl and enjoy it.

Recipe#8 Alkaline Vegan Keto Health Freak Smoothie

This smoothie is the perfect recipe to fill you up and help you stay energized for hours.

Servings: 2
Ingredients
Liquid:
- 1 cup of coconut milk
- Half cup cashew milk
- 2 teaspoons coconut oil

Dry:
- 1 big avocado, peeled, pitted and sliced
- Half lemon, peeled and sliced
- A handful of cashews
- A handful of almonds

Other:
- 1 teaspoon spirulina
- Himalayan salt to taste

Instructions:
1. Place all the ingredients in a blender.
2. Process until smooth.
3. Serve in a smoothie glass and garnish with a few lime slices.
4. Drink to your health, and enjoy!

Recipe #9 Sweet But Super Alkaline Smoothie

This smoothie is great as a quick energizing snack or even as a dessert.

Serves: 1-2
Ingredients
Liquid:

- 1 cup unsweetened coconut milk (or coconut yogurt, must be vegan without)
- 1 tablespoon coconut oil

Dry:

- 2 small limes, peeled and cut into smaller pieces
- 1-inch ginger, peeled
- 1 tablespoon chia seeds

Other:

- 1 teaspoon cinnamon powder
- Optional: stevia to sweeten

Instructions

1. Place all the ingredients in a blender.
2. Process well until smooth.
3. If needed, sweeten with stevia.

100% Alkaline Smoothie Recipes

Recipe #10 Vitamin C Happy Mind Smoothie

This smoothie combines spinach and grapefruits to help you enjoy more energy. Grapefruit, just like limes and lemons, is considered an alkaline-forming fruit because of its very low sugar content and high alkaline mineral profile.

Serves: 1-2
Ingredients
Liquid:
- 2 cups coconut water, unsweetened

Dry:
- 1 small avocado, peeled, pitted and sliced
- Half cup mixed greens washed
- 1 big grapefruit, peeled and cut into smaller pieces
- 2 tablespoons sunflower seeds

Instructions
1. Place all the ingredients in a blender.
2. Process well until smooth.
3. Enjoy!

Recipe #11 Alkaline Mediterranean Smoothie Meal

This recipe is similar to the original Spanish gazpacho recipe. It also sneaks in some greens, healthy fats, and alkaline friendly protein. All vegan alkaline and awesome!

Serves: 2
Ingredients
Liquid:
- 2 cups water, filtered, preferably alkaline
- Half cup cashew or almond milk
- 2 tablespoons extra virgin, organic olive oil (or avocado oil)

Dry:
- 3 big tomatoes, roughly chopped
- A handful of almonds, soaked in water for at least a few hours
- 2 big cucumbers, peeled
- 2 slices of lime, peel removed
- 5 small radishes
- 1 big green bell pepper, roughly chopped
- A few onion rings
- 2 garlic cloves, peeled

100% Alkaline Smoothie Recipes

Other:
- 2 generous pinches of Himalayan salt
- Half teaspoon oregano
- Half teaspoon black pepper
- Half teaspoon basil (or a few fresh basil leaves)
- Half teaspoon parsley (or a few fresh parsley leaves)

To serve:
- 1-2 tablespoons fresh lemon juice to serve
- 1-2 tablespoons chopped chive to serve

Instructions:
1. Place all the ingredients in a blender.
2. Process well until smooth.
3. Taste to see if you need to add any more herbs, spices, or Himalayan salt.
4. Serve in a small soup bowl, adding in some fresh lemon juice and fresh chive.
5. Enjoy!

Recipe #12 Sexy Chia Seed Smoothie

This simple alkaline vegan smoothie is based mostly on herbs and spices. Oh, and some chia seeds!

Serves: 1-2
Ingredients
- 1 cup coconut milk, unsweetened
- Juice of 1 lime

Dry:
- 1 tablespoon chia seeds
- A handful of cashews

Other:
- Half teaspoon cinnamon powder
- 1 generous pinch of nutmeg powder
- A few fresh mint leaves

Instructions:
1. Place all the ingredients in a blender.
2. Process until smooth.
3. Now, try the smoothie to see if you like the taste.
4. If needed, add in some stevia and blend again.
5. Place in a smoothie glass, drink, and enjoy!

Recipe #13 Spicy Alkaline Smoothie Meal Replacement

This smoothie is spicy, nourishing, comforting, and filling. Perfect for a quick lunch or dinner!

Serves: 2
Ingredients
Liquid:
- 1 cup of coconut milk
- 1 cup water, filtered, preferably alkaline

Dry:
- 2 sweet potatoes, peeled and cooked
- 1 big tomato, cut into smaller pieces
- A few onion rings
- 1 big garlic clove, peeled
- 1-inch turmeric, peeled (use gloves unless you want to end up with naturally orange fingers and nails for a couple of days)
- 2 tablespoons raw almonds, soaked in water for at least a few hours

Other:
- A big handful of fresh cilantro leaves washed
- A big handful of fresh parsley leaves washed

- A generous pinch of Himalayan salt
- A pinch red chili powder
- A pinch cumin powder
- A pinch black pepper powder
- 1 tablespoon extra-virgin, organic olive oil or avocado oil (cold-pressed)
- 1 tablespoon lime juice, to serve

Instructions
1. Place all the ingredients in a blender.
2. Process until smooth.
3. Serve in a big smoothie glass or a soup bowl.
4. Sprinkle over some lime juice and enjoy!

Recipe #14 Quinoa Alkaline Protein Smoothie

Quinoa makes this smoothie super-filling and adds some natural protein.

Serves: 1-2
Ingredients
Liquid:
- 1 cup coconut milk, unsweetened
- Juice of 1 lemon

Dry:
- 5 big tablespoons of quinoa, cooked and cooled down
- 1 big cucumber, peeled and cut into smaller pieces
- 1 small garlic clove, peeled

Other:
- A big handful of cilantro leaves washed
- A pinch of Himalayan salt
- A pinch of cumin powder
- A pinch of curry powder

Instructions
1. Blend all the ingredients in a blender.
2. Serve and enjoy!

100% Alkaline Smoothie Recipes

Recipe #15 Spicy Green Aphrodisiac Smoothie

Arugula is one of my favorite alkaline superfoods! It's very rich in calcium and iron as well as vitamin A, and it tastes great in smoothies!

Serves: 1-2
Ingredients
Liquid:
- 1 cup of coconut milk
- 1 cup rooibos tea infusion, cooled down

Dry:
- 1 cup fresh arugula leaves, washed
- A handful of fresh parsley leaves, washed
- A handful of cilantro leaves, washed
- 1 tablespoon chia seeds or chia seed powder

Other:
- A pinch of Himalayan salt
- A pinch of chili powder
- A pinch of black pepper powder
- A pinch of oregano

Instructions
1. Place all the ingredients in a blender.
2. Blend well until smooth.
3. Serve in a smoothie glass and enjoy!

Recipe #16 When Life Throws Lemons Smoothie

This smoothie is just perfect on a hot summer day. It will help you stay refreshed and energized. Oh, and it's all alkaline vegan!

Serves: 2-3
Ingredients
Liquid:
- 1 cup almond milk
- 1 cup of coconut water

Dry:
- 2 small limes, peeled and cut into smaller pieces
- 2 tablespoons chia seeds

Other:
- 1 teaspoon cinnamon powder
- 1 cup of ice cubes
- Stevia to sweeten, if needed

Instructions:
1. Place everything in a blender.
2. Process until smooth. Serve and enjoy!
3. Serve chilled and enjoy! This smoothie also makes a great morning detox drink.

Recipe #17 Irresistible Satisfaction Smoothie

Parsley is a highly alkaline-forming ingredient, an excellent source of vitamins K and C as well as a good source of vitamin A, and iron. Tomato juice is very alkaline-forming because tomato is low sugar and high nutrient fruit.

Serves: 2-3
Ingredients
Liquid:
- 1 cup of organic tomato juice
- 1 cup of coconut milk

Dry:
- A handful of almonds, soaked overnight
- 2 big sweet potatoes, cooked and peeled
- 1 small zucchini, peeled and slightly cooked or steamed

Other:
- Half cup parsley leaves, washed
- A pinch of Himalayan salt
- A pinch of black pepper

Instructions
1. Place all the ingredients in a blender.
2. Process well until smooth.
3. Enjoy!

Recipe #18 Sweet Sleep Princess Alkaline Smoothie

This smoothie is designed to help you relax and sleep better.

Serves: 1- 2
Ingredients
Liquid
- 1 cup of chamomile infusion (use 1 teabag per cup), cooled
- 1 cup almond milk

Dry:
- 1 small avocado, peeled and seeded
- A few lime and lemon slices

Other:
- A pinch of Himalayan salt
- A pinch of nutmeg

Instructions
1. Combine all the ingredients in a blender.
2. Process well until smooth.
3. Serve and enjoy!

Recipe #19 Herbs Are Awesome Smoothie

This smoothie uses horsetail infusion, a natural remedy aimed at reducing water retention and speeding up detoxification. All herbal, caffeine-free infusions are very alkaline and can also be used in smoothies.

Serves: 2
Ingredients
Liquid:
- 1 cup horsetail infusion, cooled down (use 1 tea bag per cup)
- Half cup fresh grapefruit juice

Dry:
- 1-inch ginger
- 2 tablespoons chia seed powder
- Half avocado, peeled and seeded

Other:
- 1 teaspoon cinnamon powder
- 1 teaspoon vanilla powder

Instructions
1. Blend all the ingredients in a blender.
2. Serve in a smoothie glass and enjoy!

Recipe #20 Creamy Glow Alkaline Smoothie

Cucumbers rich in vitamin C and vitamin A as well as alkaline minerals such as magnesium, potassium, and manganese. Nice, soft and refreshing alkaline superfoods that taste great in smoothies!

Serves: 1-2
Ingredients
Liquid:
- 1 cup mint tea, cooled down
- 1 cup coconut or cashew milk
- 1 tablespoon coconut oil

Dry:
- 2 big cucumbers, peeled and sliced
- half cup fresh arugula leaves
- 1 clove garlic, peeled
- 1 tablespoon chia seed powder

Other:
- Pinch of black pepper
- Pinch of Himalayan salt
- A small handful of fresh cilantro leaves to garnish

Instructions:
1. Place in a blender and process until smooth.
2. Garnish with fresh cilantro, serve and enjoy!

100% Alkaline Smoothie Recipes

Recipe #21 Anti-Inflammatory Power Alkaline Smoothie

This smoothie is an excellent natural remedy to boost your immune system.

Serves: 1-2
Ingredients
Liquid:
- 1 cup of coconut water
- 1 cup fennel tea (cooled down)

Dry:
- 2-inches ginger washed and peeled
- 2-inches turmeric washed and peeled
- 1 big cucumber, peeled and chopped
- Half an avocado pitted
- A few lemon slices, peeled

Other:
- A few ice cubes
- Himalayan salt to taste
- Pinch of chili powder
- Pinch of black pepper

Instructions:
1. Place everything in a blender and process until smooth.
2. Serve and enjoy!

Recipe #22 Sweet Herbal Dream Alkaline Smoothie

Fennel tea tastes delicious in a smoothie when combined with naturally creamy, alkaline plant-based milk.

Serves: 1-2
Ingredients
Liquid:
- 1 cup fennel tea (use 1 fennel tea bag per 1 cup of boiling water), cooled down
- Half cup coconut milk, unsweetened

Dry:
- 1 grapefruit, peeled and cut into smaller pieces
- Half avocado, peeled and pitted
- 1-inch ginger, peeled

Other:
- A few mint leaves to garnish
- A few ice cubes to serve
- Optional: stevia to sweeten

Instructions:
1. Place all the ingredients in a blender.
2. Process well until smooth.
3. Garnish with mint leaves, serve and enjoy!

Recipe #23 Rooibos Energy Smoothie

Rooibos is considered an alkaline tea, because of its high mineral and antioxidant content. And it makes your alkaline vegan smoothies super nutritious!

Serves: 2
Ingredients
Liquid:
- 1 cup of rooibos tea, cooled down (use 1 teabag per cup)
- Half cup almond or coconut milk

Dry:
- 1-inch ginger, peeled
- 1 -inch turmeric, peeled (orange nails- remember to get kitchen gloves...)
- 1 big grapefruit, peeled and cut into smaller chunks
- 1 teaspoon chia seeds

Other:
- 1 teaspoon spirulina powder

Instructions:
1. Place all the ingredients in a blender.
2. Process well until smooth.
3. Serve and enjoy!

100% Alkaline Smoothie Recipes

Recipe #24 Veggies Taste Awesome Smoothie

Veggie smoothies always work well on the alkaline vegan diet. To make them taste amazing, all we need are some herbs and spices.

Serves: 2
Ingredients
Liquid:
- 1 cup tomato juice
- Juice of 2 limes
- Half cup of coconut milk
- Optional: water (filtered, preferably alkaline) if needed

Dry:
- 1 big zucchini, peeled, raw or steamed
- 1 cup artichoke hearts, cooked
- 2 garlic cloves, peeled

Other:
- A generous pinch of Himalayan salt
- A pinch of black pepper
- A pinch of chili and curry powder (optional)
- Optional: A few cilantro leaves to garnish

Instructions:
1. Place all the ingredients in a blender.
2. Process until smooth.
3. If needed, add some water and process again.
4. Serve and enjoy!

100% Alkaline Smoothie Recipes

Recipe #25 Fill Me Up Easy Lunch Smoothie

Garlic and ginger add to the anti-inflammatory and immune system boosting properties of this super alkaline smoothie.

Serves: 2
Ingredients
Liquid:
- 1 cup almond milk
- 1 cup water, filtered, preferable alkaline
- 1 tablespoon avocado or olive oil

Dry:
- 2 red bell peppers, chopped
- 4 tomatoes, cut into smaller pieces
- 1 small garlic clove, peeled
- 2 inches ginger, peeled
- 1 tablespoon hemp seed protein powder

Other:
- Pinch of Himalayan salt to taste
- Pinch of black pepper to taste

Instructions:
1. Blend all the ingredients in a blender.
2. Serve in a smoothie glass or a small soup bowl. Enjoy!

Recipe #26 No-Guilt Healthy Alkaline Vegan Treat Smoothie

This smoothie is healthy, natural treat you can turn to whenever you are craving something sweet. And it's all alkaline vegan!

Serves: 1-2
Ingredients
Liquid:
- 1 cup thick coconut milk, unsweetened
- 1 tablespoon coconut oil

Dry:
- A big handful of almonds, soaked in water for at least a few hours
- 2 tablespoons chia seeds

Other:
- Optional: stevia to sweeten
- 1 teaspoon cinnamon powder
- Half teaspoon Ashwagandha powder

Instructions:
1. Place all the ingredients in a blender.
2. Process well until smooth.
3. Serve chilled and enjoy!

Recipe #27 Relax Your Body, Mind, and Soul Smoothie

Ashwagandha is known as an adaptogenic herb. Adaptogens are known to help the body cope with and fight against external stressors such as toxins and the environment, as well as internal stressors such as anxiety and insomnia and depression.

Serves: 1-2
Ingredients
Liquid:
- 1 cup almond milk
- 1 cup cashew milk

Dry:
- 2 small carrots, peeled
- 1 tablespoon chia seeds
- Half avocado, peeled and pitted

Other:
- A handful of shredded coconut
- Half teaspoon Ashwagandha powder

Instructions
1. Blend everything together until smooth.
2. Serve in a smoothie glass and enjoy!

Recipe #28 The New Spanish Alkaline Smoothie

This smoothie tastes great while offering a myriad of good fats, chlorophyll-rich, healing greens, and natural protein. All you need to enjoy vibrant, alkaline vegan health!

Serves: 2
Ingredients
Liquid:
- 1 cup almond milk
- 1 tablespoon extra-virgin, cold-pressed olive oil

Dry:
- 2 medium-sized cucumbers, peeled and chopped
- 1 big garlic clove, peeled
- 1 avocado, peeled and pitted
- A handful of fresh spinach
- A handful of raw cashews, soaked in water for at least a few hours

Other:
- Pinch of Himalayan salt
- Pinch of black pepper

Instructions
1. Place all the ingredients in a blender and process until smooth.
2. Serve in a smoothie glass or a small soup bowl.
3. Enjoy!

Recipe #29 Super Effective Detox Smoothie

Celery is rich in vitamin C, fiber, alkaline minerals such as potassium and is also very hydrating and replenishing. Personally, I don't find it very tasty. But I know it's good for me, so I decided to experiment and combine it with other green alkaline ingredients I like.

Serves: 2
Ingredients:
Liquid:
- 1 cup tomato juice
- 1 cup cashew or think coconut milk
- 1 tablespoon of flaxseed or avocado oil

Dry:
- A small handful of celery leaves
- A small handful of cilantro leaves (+ a few extra to garnish)
- A small handful of parsley leaves
- A few fresh mint leaves

Other:
- Himalayan salt and black pepper to taste

Instructions:
1. Place all the ingredients in a blender and process until smooth.
2. Serve and enjoy!

Recipe #30 Cinnamon Aphrodisiac Smoothie

Arugula is a natural aphrodisiac, and so is the cinnamon. Chia seeds make this smoothie even more nutritious!

Servings: 2
Ingredients:
Liquid:
- 1 cup of coconut milk

Dry:
- A handful of fresh arugula leaves, washed
- 1 tablespoon chia seeds

Other:
- 1 teaspoon cinnamon
- 1 teaspoon vanilla

Instructions:
1. Place all the ingredients through a blender.
2. Process well until smooth and creamy. If needed, add some water. Serve and enjoy!

Recipe #31 Hydration Refreshment Alkaline Protein Smoothie

Almonds are high in protein, good fats, and fiber and make your alkaline vegan smoothies more nutritious. Perfect as a quick, morning smoothie.

Servings:2
Ingredients
Liquid:
- 1 cup of coconut milk
- 1 cup water, filtered, preferably alkaline

Dry:
- Half cup arugula leaves
- A handful of almonds, soaked in water for at least a few hours
- 1 grapefruit, peeled

Other:
- 1 teaspoon nutmeg powder
- 1 teaspoon cinnamon powder

Instructions:
1. Place all the ingredients through a blender.
2. Process, serve, and enjoy!

Recipe #32 Easy Sweet Green Smoothie

If you are having a hard time drinking green smoothies, this recipe will help fall in love with greens. It's very alkaline and super creamy.

Servings: 2
Ingredients
Liquid:
- 1 cup of coconut water
- 1 cup rooibos tea, cooled down

Dry:
- 1 big avocado, peeled and pitted
- 1 tablespoon chia seeds
- A few lime slices, peeled

Other:
- 1 tablespoon cinnamon powder
- A few drops of liquid chlorophyll

Instructions:
1. Place all the ingredients through a blender.
2. Process well until smooth and creamy.
3. Serve and enjoy!

100% Alkaline Smoothie Recipes

Karen's personal email is:

karenveganbooks@gmail.com

Always happy to connect with you,
With love and light,
Karen

Special Free Offer from Karen- VIP Reader Newsletter

Are you looking for more vegan health inspiration?

Join my **free email newsletter** today and start receiving my best vegan tips, recipes, and resources:

Visit:
www.YourWellnessBooks.com/karen

to sign up now.

(As my VIP reader, you will be the first one to learn about my new books at super discounted prices + giveaways +discounts).

Join now, it's free:

www.YourWellnessBooks.com/karen

I am looking forward to connecting with you, helping you on your journey.

More Books by Karen Greenvang

Pegan Diet Cookbook

Alkaline Vegan Drinks

Vegan Baking

Spiralizer Cookbook

Vegan Protein Smoothies & Green Smoothies

And many more books and eBooks available at:

www.amazon.com/author/karengreenvang

Bonus Content - Alkaline Acid Food Lists

The following charts are based on Doctor Robert O-Young's latest research.

They show you the alkalizing /acidifying effect that different foods have on your body after they have been consumed (not before).

Many websites will list charts that are not accurate- they determine acidity or alkalinity on the food before it is consumed. So the results can be pretty confusing, especially for a newbie...

Alkaline Veggies:
- Asparagus
- Broccoli
- Chilli
- Capsicum/Pepper
- Courgette/Zucchini
- Dandelion
- Cabbage
- Sweet Potato
- Mint
- Ginger

- Coriander
- Basil
- Brussels Sprouts
- Pumpkin
- Radish
- Snowpeas
- Green Beans
- String Beans
- Runner Beans
- Spinach
- Kale
- Cauliflower
- Carrot
- Beetroot
- Eggplant/Aubergine
- Garlic
- Onion
- Parsley
- Butternut etc.)
- Pumpkin
- Wakame
- Kelp
- Collards
- Chives
- Endive

- Chard
- Celery
- Cucumber
- Watercress
- Lettuce
- Peas
- Broad Beans
- New Potato

ALKALINE SPROUTS:
- Soy Sprouts
- Alfalfa Sprouts
- Amaranth Sprouts
- Broccoli Sprouts
- Fenugreek Sprouts
- Kamut Sprouts
- Mung Bean Sprouts
- Quinoa Sprouts
- Radish Sprouts
- Spelt Sprout

ALKALINE FRUITS:
- Avocado
- Tomato
- Lemon
- Lime
- Grapefruit
- Fresh Coconut
- Pomegranate

ALKALINE GRASSES:
- Wheatgrass
- Barley Grass
- Kamut Grass
- Dog Grass
- Shave Grass
- Oat Grass

ALKALINE NUTS AND SEEDS:
- Almonds
- Coconut
- Flax Seeds
- Pumpkin Seeds
- Sesame Seeds
- Sunflower Seeds

ALKALINE OILS:
- Avocado Oil
- Coconut Oil
- Flax Oil
- Udo's Oil
- Olive Oil

ALKALINE bread:
- Sprouted Bread
- Sprouted Wraps
- Gluten/Yeast
- Free Breads & Wraps

ALKALINE BEANS AND GRAINS
- Amaranth
- Buckwheat
- Chia/Salba
- Kamut
- Millet
- Quinoa
- Lentils
- Mung Beans
- Pinto Beans
- Red Beans
- Soy Beans
- White Beans

ACID FRUIT (much less acidic than meat, in fact, many fruits are <u>neutral- moderately acidic</u> so don't try to eliminate them, don't get too paranoid about fruit, simply check what works for you and try to eat more alkaline fruits and veggies):

- Apple
- Apricot
- Currants
- Dates
- Grapes
- Currants
- Honeydew Melon
- Mango
- Peach
- Pear
- Prunes
- Raisins
- Orange
- Pineapple
- Plum
- Raspberries
- Strawberries
- Tropical Fruits
- Cantaloupe
- Cranberries

- Plum

ALL MEATS/FISH ARE ACID-FORMING
- Oyster
- Pork
- Rabbit
- Sausage
- Scallops
- Shellfish
- Shrimp
- Veal
- Bacon
- Beef
- Clams
- Corned Beef
- Eggs
- Lamb
- Organ Meats
- Venison
- Fish
- Lobster

SO ARE EGGS/DAIRY:
- Butter
- Cheese
- Milk
- Whey
- Yogurt
- Cottage Cheese
- Ice Cream
- Sour Cream
- Soy Cheese
- Eggs

CAFFEINE/ENERGY DRINKS/ARTIFICIAL SWEETENERS AND OTHER ACIDIC FOODS AND DRINKS:
- Saccharine
- Sucrose
- Sucralose
- Honey
- Maple SyrupAlcohol
- Black Tea
- Coffee
- Carbonated Water
- Pasteurized Juice
- Cocoa

- Energy Drinks
- Sports Drinks
- Colas
- Tap Water
- Milk
- Green Tea
- Decaffeinated Drinks
- Flavoured Water
- Artificial Sweeteners
- Carob
- Corn Syrup
- Fructose
- Processed Sugar
- Mayonnaise
- Ketchup
- Mustard
- Soy Sauce
- Pickles
- Vinegar
- Tabasco
- Tamari
- Wasabi

ACID OILS AND OTHER:
- Cooked Oil
- Solid Oil (Margarine)
- Oil Exposed to Heat,
- Light or Air
- Mushrooms
- Miso
- White Bread, Pasta,
- Rice & Noodles
- Chocolate
- Chips
- Pizza
- Biscuits
- Cigarettes
- Drugs
- Candy!

Scientific Resources

More resources, research and scientific proof that advocates increasing your consumption of alkaline-friendly foods

Article Title: Alkaline Mineral Supplementation Decreases Pain in Rheumatoid Arthritis Patients: A Pilot Study
Article Published: The Open Nutrition Journal, 2008, 2, 100-105
Authors: Regina Maria Cseuz, Istvan Barna, Tamas Bender, and Jürgen Vormann

Article Title: Does correction of metabolic acidosis slow chronic kidney disease progression?
Article Published: Current Opinion in Nephrology & Hypertension: March 2013 – Volume 22 – Issue 2 – p 193–197
Authors: Goraya, N; Wesson, D.

Article Title: Dietary Acid Load and Metabolic Acidosis in Renal Transplant Recipients
Article Published: Clinical Journal of the American Society of Nephrology November 07, 2012, vol. 7 no. 11 1811-1818
Authors: Else van den Berg

Article Title: Acid–base balance may influence risk for insulin resistance syndrome by modulating cortisol output
Article Published: Medical Hypotheses Volume 64, Issue 2, 2005, Pages 380–384
Authors: Mark F. McCarty

Article Title: The Acid-Base Hypothesis: Diet and Bone in the Framingham Osteoporosis Study
Article Published: European Journal of Nutrition October 2001, Volume 40, Issue 5, pp 231-237
Authors: Tucker KL, Hannan M, Douglas P

Article Title: Effect of a supplement rich in alkaline minerals on acid-base balance in humans
Article Published: Nutrition Journal 2009, 8:23
Authors: Daniel König, Klaus Muser, Hans-Hermann Dickhuth, Aloys Berg and Peter Deibert

www.ingramcontent.com/pod-product-compliance
Lightning Source LLC
Chambersburg PA
CBHW071746080526
44588CB00013B/2167